waterline war paint

by
Flora Marrugi

Janelle & Craig,

Thanks so much for the support ♥ You guys are so amazing I'm glad met you both and can call you friends ♥

waterline war paint

2

to every friend, past and present
you comforted me when i needed it the most
when i forgot my own self worth
you were there to remind me, i deserved more

thank you

waterline war paint

*the five*

there are five types of people you will meet in
the world of dating:

*the first love*
    i was completely naïve and you were just
    a snowflake in this storm
*the cheater*
    i learned a valuable lesson with you-
    always trust your gut
*the one you met too soon*
    if i met you later on in life it would have
    ended differently
*the one you always go back to*
    you were a fairytale- i continually waited
*the one that completely breaks you*
    you were the storm that froze me
    the only one i hope, as well as dread, for
    the day you come back to me

some will meet all five in one person, while
others experience them in multiplies. we walk in
blindly hoping for nothing more than to fall
madly in love and receive a happy ending. we
learn the hard way that life doesn't work that
way. i promise, you'll be okay.

waterline war paint

to my five,

it was a new norm
shielding myself from meteors
yes, you each shot right through and left a part of
me hollow
i regrew and placed all five rocks on a shelf in
the form of words leading to my new motto
turn the page, and see what follows


i heard you swallow

waterline war paint

waterline war paint


the first ache

i never understood how girls would fall
how could someone meet another and let their
life come to an instant halt?
questioning, is that life's curveball?
i read about love stories in books
romeo and juliet, what a terrible hook
listened to songs on how i should dive head first
allow one to fill my thirst
a kiss to end all those who've felt cursed
your lips, the first line to this endless verse

waterline war paint

we danced in the parking lot
your car stereo played our favorite love song
in a short amount of time
you swept me off my feet
i let myself fall in love with every spin
two left feet creating this loves prologue

a good morning text goes a long way
two simple words create a virtual bouquet
smile and blush to begin the day
never thought i'd wake up to such a sweet bay

i held our love high for all to see
so proud of our story
pranced you around, indulging in the glory
i wore your name, a dangling key
the girl i once knew myself to be
was nowhere in sight
the new me was the lead in this eight-month
movie

i argued and fought, defending our flowerpot
against any who destined us with drought

under a blossoming apple-tree
we laid in the breeze
spoke of dreams and what we were to be
while the sun stood high
it peeked through the leaves
gently glistening the skin of my bare thigh
we spoke of years to come
not knowing it would only last a couple months

hand in hand we sketched our names in the sand
felt the warm breeze across my skin
your hand gently brushing my hair behind my
ear
the brown in your eyes became a promised land
each kiss as strong as sin
whispers only i can hear

feel me here
feel me there
feel me where your hands should be

you held me close to your chest
you said you loved me
you told me that this was forever
your definition of forever was different from
mine

i trusted you
i gave you everything
i believed in you
i believed in us
my heart danced at the sound of your name
i never saw an end
who would have thought it was all pretend

mascara on my pillow
once on my eyes
already know the eyeliner on my waterline
created a trail down this face of mine
you said goodbye
on the day you were meant to be my valentine

phone ringing, constantly worried friends
sending messages back, *"please just let me be"*
holding the bear i got on christmas eve
i closed my eyes and tried to sleep

you left no trace behind
a ghost left haunting my world
it's not you who needs to follow the light
your world is not the dark one

i'd rather not think of you
doing so brings an undesirable amount of pain
chest begins to darken
while my soul begins to cry
all this hidden underneath
so deeply away under this blue sky

i feel so empty inside
so hollow and fragile
you ignited a flame within me
i am consumed with fumes left behind from the
candle you blew out
no emotion
no cares
empty

i dug a hole in what was once our soil
placed the pendant underneath
covered it with words and rain from august
i should have covered it in concrete
your love was the kind that a girl should never
repeat

to think about it made my heart thump
starts to make horrendous noises
to speak about it brought trembles to my voice
started to sound like a scratched record
to continue living i thought would bring an
unimaginable amount of pain
who was i to think that there would be nothing
from this to gain

waterline war paint

the pain was visible in my eyes
a smile hid the girl who cried last night
you were only the first of many goodbyes

waterline war paint

waterline war paint


number two

oh, i'm your number two?
this one's for you
don't flatter yourself
you're still irrelevant
this chapter is only to warn others of those like
you


by the way, i finally found a use for all your
pointless text messages ☺

you claimed to taste like poetry on a morning
flight
you said your heart was where i should land
forgiving once seemed so easy, but your lies
proved that to be wrong
soft and gentle touch
like an ocean breathing once it seeing the
morning sun

text received 6:00am
*"good morning cutie ;)"*

your lingering smell is much like a spell
i've never been much of a damsel
yet you had me hooked like bait
i never expected a backlash

text received 2:10am
*"you up? i wanna hear your voice."*

waterline war paint

it was always hidden spots
unvisited coffee shops
dates in your car
never once thinking they were bizarre
meeting me once the movie starts
your way of hiding us, oh what a fine art

text received 3:00pm
*"i just don't think we need a label."*

six months in, still haven't met a single friend
yet, i heard stories of each mischievous weekend
your late-night phone calls became a noticeable
trend
i was playing pretend to avoid a bitter end
delaying made no sense when this street was
always a dead-end

text received 1:10pm
*"i have to work late tonight. it's so busy i'll text
you once i leave."*

did you expect me to not believe my best friend?
you never mentioned you had a girlfriend
then again, it all made sense
the plot has thickened, building crowd suspense
darling, you wrote this setting
let the scene commence

text received 2:50pm
*"i swear i don't even know her."*

doing what i did was far from petty
she deserved more than a rotten penny
three-way call stung like covering a wound with
alcohol
we both let you go and watched you fall

text received 1:50pm
*"i've been with her for so long i didn't know
how to end it."*

i felt it go straight through
i felt it disturb every beat
it straining my ability to breathe
i felt it tearing apart the previous wounds
gasped as it created those anew
i felt it scream silent tears
held my breath, hoping to ease the pain
i felt it pound a hole right through my chest
you triggered tears of acid rain

text received 2:10am
*"i'm so sorry. i never meant to hurt you."*

i let you make me feel small
beaten and broken, barely able to crawl
i was the pin and you the bowling ball
refusing to answer your 27th missed call

text received 1:00pm
*"i miss you. please pick up."*

you created such insecurity it haunts my every
thought
questioning motives and doubting their choice
for everyone after you will never see the me
before
convincing myself i'm worthy was never a daily
chore

text received 1:40pm
*"please talk to me."*

just thinking of your name lights my skin on fire
you're the image of a perfect liar
wearing a golden cross, putting shame to the
choir
are you proud of using my desire to get by my
barb wires?
reminding me to build my wall a little bit higher
it's those like you causing hopeless romantics to
retire

text received 4:00pm
*"i miss you so much. can we still be friends?"*

yes, losing you hurt
but that's not the part that's the worst
feeling as if i'm not good enough
was my love that easy to give up?
coming in second taught me a lesson
those who care won't use your heart as a weapon

text received 2:50pm
*"hello?"*

there's a special playlist i created just for you
many of the songs feature two specific words
in those moments i'm feeling blue
*shuffle and play*
how absurd of me to feel an ounce of grey


*playlist-fuck you*
*164 songs*


text received 2:50am
*"can't sleep. you're all i'm thinking about."*

there are times i zone out
continuous driving, forgetting my route
it replays like a broken record
i never asked for an encore
swallow this pain like a pill
heart running on diesel

text received 1:50pm
*"please talk to me. i feel like shit."*

i didn't know what it felt like to be an option till
you came around
this heart became your personal playground
stood on your never-ending merry-go-round
i wasn't waiting to be the winner
leaped off, landing on my knees
i'd rather let these wood chips be my splinter

text received 2:10pm
*"she left me but i always wanted you."*

i woke up to your words etched into my skin
i never planned on being placed on an easel
thread and needle, on display for people

text received 3:00am
*"please give me a second chance"*

i felt each snowflake on my skin
you spun me hopelessly, wanting me to forgive
in the middle of a snowstorm, you cursed all the
pain, hoping i would bid it farewell into the
abyss
it was your kiss that now felt like a sin
reminding me

i deserve more than a love so thin

text received 8:00pm
*"you're the only one i want now."*

you see my face from time to time
  *"you look really good. it feels like it's
  been a lifetime"*

ordering my whiskey sour
thinking of how stupid of me to ever want to be
called your flower

text received 5:00pm
*"my biggest regret in life was losing you"*

the most lovable people are the ones who don't
want to be loved again
maybe that's why we become so fixated with
them
we want to hold them
let our arms whisper comfort
allow our skin to heal their wounds

for me, that person will never be you



text sent 5:27pm
*"it's been two years. i've been over you"*

like i said, you'll always be irrelevant

waterline war paint

dear boston

i'll board a plane
take a strong leap of faith
to see you once again
passion running through each vein
hopeless romantic freeing my wings in a new
lane

in front of me, you stand
flowers in hand
a smile on your face
my heart dancing to an enjoyable pace

we roamed the streets covered in art
held my hand tightly
watching me put my head back and laugh
unknowingly stealing your heart

it was in your eyes i found love
it was in your eyes i saw a future
it was in your eyes i felt a warmth
it was in your eyes i fell

as the night begins to fade
i'll rest my gaze upon the shade of green that
hides within your eyes
because that is where the sun will always rise

oh, how beautiful you look tonight
rest your head
as my arms build a fort
your troubles, they are mine
let's just keep this night divine

this, a risk a girl should take
a kiss so soft it could build athenas thrown
they're rooting for this love to burn at the stake
shield set for any who dare to throw a stone

we got in the car and began to drive
no plan in sight
nothing more than a road and the time we arrive
my spontaneous love filled knight

we stood in the center of the city
running on five hours of sleep
the time of night has yet to hit me
smiles and laughter in the back of a taxi
you were everything i wished for

*everything, exactly*

you held my hand in the back of the taxi
i felt your pulse beating rapidly, attempting to
catch up to me
i felt like a lost fish being brought back to sea
missing a few scales
yet my colors were all you could see
there we were on broadway and worth
thinking to myself, our love will only go north


*locked our love in manhattan*

you give me unplausible reasons
if i have any doubt
i hope you fill them with love filled grout

if i could go back, i would
i'd tell myself *"your insecurities are no-good"*
young love is so fragile
the crackling of a short candle
we met way too soon
wondering, if we met now would it even be a
battle

i was afraid of how perfect this was
i was afraid of the possibility of getting hurt
unknowingly, i created a night that would haunt
me
i cried on the edge of my seat
as you tried to comfort me

waterline war paint

here it comes
the lump in my throat
i sit in front of you fiddling my thumbs
unable to say the words
knowing they soon will haunt both our worlds

i drove off
your eyes were all i thought of
those tears, the underlining of this black plague
horn honking behind me
i didn't notice the red light
this heartbreak was a new height

it wasn't you
it's the bastard who took my heart
smashed it
then burned it to ashes

saying i don't miss you would be a lie
you were my person
it's just a part of me felt like you weren't meant
to be mine

you gave me nothing but memories i'll forever
hold on to
please believe me when I say
for me, you'll never fade away

i wish for you to forget me
not because i never cared
only so you can find someone that will love you
much more than i promised you

saying i miss you wouldn't be fair
i hurt you
i saw it in your eyes

*i never want to see that pain again*

dear boston,

i was crazy for letting you go
i knew that the moment those words came out
a part of me hopes that you know that
considering the fact that tears were running
down my face on that second night
i felt like i wasn't enough
i felt like i would never give you what you
deserve
i know so many say that
that so many use that as an excuse
but it's true
i felt like complete shit after
what we had was real
i was just so worried that i wasn't the best for
you
so worried that i let go of the only person who
made me feel like the only one on the dance
floor
i'll always have to dismiss wanting to give you
another goldfish kiss

waterline war paint

i'm sorry

waterline war paint

waterline war paint

blonde and blue

you found me in this virtual world
from day one you took me on a whirl
eyes stuck like glue
such a hypnotizing blue
i lost all sense of time
what did i get myself into

the whiskey on your lips was ever so sweet
the cigarette ashes on your tongue were never
too much for me

your confidence grasped me
your ability to stand strong enlightened me
your way of reassuring me was the key
this love, a continuous repeat

there we were, hidden between the trees
the smell of pine in the midnight breeze
found a place on my tongue
every time our lips would seize
i've surrendered to my knees


*aiming to please*

there's a part of me that can't let you go
the same part of me that still gives you hope
there's a part of me that wants to know
i no longer want to wait
for you to choose if you'll stay or go

if you decide to shower me with devotion
i'll welcome it with open arms
but, don't think for a second that i'll be crying
over your ungiven charms

i've danced as it rained a thousand knives
i felt no guilt in choosing to love you so

rough on the outside
soft from within
part of me felt the hidden you
whenever i looked into your shades of blue

if you want me to be in your life
just hold me
rest with me tonight

in those desperate times of measure
you can open up to me
i'll make you full of pleasure as you lay on top
of me


*salty sweet disposition*

you shoulda been there
you shoulda been strong
you shoulda been there to prove me wrong

i can't hold my breath for someone who's too afraid to turn the page

*tick tock*

breathe like sin, mixed with a little gin
there's a story behind that mischievous grin
must have been your thumb grazing my skin
leading me to believe there was no end to our
begin


*my personal deadly sin*

for a moment, i could picture our world
evening gowns, frosted in pearls
discreet winks only i can see
sipping your vodka, eyes still on me
the touch of your thumb gliding over my cheek
a world where you're with me, so to speak

when you needed a taste of love
you knew where to find me
blindly thinking to myself
    *"this is what they speak of"*

my lips would cave in
thinking they finally became your safe haven
when i was only satisfying a craving

i was a girl looking for one to share my love
the kind that everyone dreamt of
how foolish of you to think
i'd wait for me to become the one you think the
world of
darling, you lost me just like a glove

phone pressed to my ear, hand shaking
sitting in my car suffocating
i heard your voice breaking
   *"i should have never kept you waiting"*


did you feel my heart aching?

our conversation ended with a *"goodnight"*
our sun had set with no moonlight in sight
no constellation to guide
eyes blind from frostbite
we were two stars never meant to collide

*"this was meant to last. i should have told you sooner. i never pictured you only a part of my past"*

i never thought we'd say goodbye
take me back to that first night in july
my stomach occupied with butterflies
just you and i

my blonde and blue sunshine

waterline war paint




you were seven years too late

waterline war paint

boy from the alley

low key, i knew you were far from safety
thinking, maybe you'd be the one to save me
in reality, you would be the one to break me

you stood next to me in the crowd
the love interest defined in books
tall and handsome, eyes like the sea
little did i know you were a storm cloud
a kiss on second and cass was all it took
watching you leave, a memory you'll forever be

dimpled and easy-hearted man
feeling your love like a sun kiss tan
smile so sweet
i sense the warmth from your hands
running through my body like pure fire
this, a girls every desire

if you want, i'll be your reason to stay
i'll give you more than i did yesterday

beat my heart till it can't gasp
hold my soul and feed it once again
i ache for your love
i only want your touch

do you see yourself how i see you?
you're the moon that shines in the night sky
you're the beating wings of a hundred fireflies
your voice a sweet lullaby
do you see yourself in such a beautiful view?


*please tell me you do*

your sky is blue, this is true
but that could all change
once you see yourself how i see you

i'll let my chest be a safe place to lay
skipping rhythm of my heart put you to sleep
these hands of mine will grasp you for life

i feel a little bit at ease
when you say that you're not going to leave
this loves too hard not to bare
hands too cold for me not to care
it's hard to see what you didn't do
when i'm falling for every move
my hearts racing and i approve
tell me what's a girl to do

a snow globe with our picture in your pocket
you and i was my favorite topic

it's such a shame how you tear down your own
hidden sparks of flame
the rain will pour until you walk to a happier
place

you only came to dally in the alley
your dreams were too big
they didn't fit this town
the people always found you in the sunrise
they didn't stop to think about your alibi

have we gone to war?
this feels like a lost battle
mascara running
a princess crying in her castle

*a broken woman's war paint*

like a shooting star
that's how fast you disappeared
was this a star-crossed love?
or more of a day that should not have seen the
morning sun

your words felt like bullets
my skin is completely scarred
i should have kept on my armor
what a fool i made of myself

*"why do you think he disappeared?"*


i wasn't good enough
that you thought there has to be someone better

my theory as to why you didn't stay

you were that rainbow in the sky
the lens on my camera failed to capture
one would have to see you in person
a photo could never do you justice

i may never be able to show one your beauty
but i can forever describe what it felt like
the moment your colors caught my eye

everything i've written was because of you
honestly, this entire book was inspired by you
the pain you caused opened up so many old
wounds
don't ever be mistaken and think i should thank
you
i hope the nights i cried curse you

i poured my heart out to you
i put it all on the line
trusted my every instinct
every bit of my inner being telling me to let you
know how even *"the thought of your name
brings joy to my day"*

i waited for your response
your four words still haunt me to this day
carved on these beating chambers that still ache

*"this was a mistake"*

no, you were a mistake

waterline war paint

hello whiskey, my new friend

what do i do when my worst flaw is loving love?
head first search to fill a wanted thirst
i've made a habit of always being the first
how did a heart wanting love become a curse?

*surviving the aftermath*

always choose you first
because if it ends it'll just be you and a text
reading *"take care of yourself"*
when what you wanted from the beginning was
someone to help you do that

it's not summertime yet i find myself curled
underneath this blanket
skin, soft to the touch
you'd never be able to tell that within lies a
tundra freezing me to my core
don't ask me why i'm so cold
why have i become so bitter?
i wore a sundress to a blizzard

the only flaw love has is that you don't get to
choose who sparks its flame
then again, is that really a flaw?

sharing your heartbreak with someone is like
trying to describe a color that doesn't exist

*why they don't understand*

if there was a way to stop myself from looking at
all our pictures together i would have already
done it
would it be wrong if i deleted them all?
am i behind? have you already done it?
that screenshot i took in the middle of your
laugh, i love it
or the one from the night before the flood hit
such a rash decision, we barely discussed this
is this a hill?
are we jack and jill without the bucket?
are you coming after me?
or should I say *'fuck it'*

sick of constant run-ins with voided ones
worse when they've found their home runs
ordering clean whiskey, easy on the rocks
lost and alone, but i've become a red fox

*adaptation.*

i've become somewhat of a game
i only have myself to blame
i let their undeserving tongues drip with the
sweetness of my name
they claim they're different
but they were all the same

my brother warned me with words that have
stuck with me till this day
make the first move
love is a chess game
remember that when you put your heart on
display


*"every person is an asshole. you just have to
find one you can put up with"*

do you realize how much makeup we waste on
those who aren't even worthy of our better than
sex?
i mean, yea they were too faced
always using that "maybe" line
honestly, they're only great lash deserving
if that
definitely, not the big brush though, let's be
honest


the only thing you brought volume to in my life
was my migraine

you will find a distraction
it will help keep your mind busy
don't worry
your tears will eventually only come from
laughter

we search for happiness
the kind that is completely effortless
internal completion
it's rare in life that such things make an
appearance
the moment it does it turns our life around
that feeling of pure happiness is beautiful
there is no word to describe it
you know it's there by the sparkle others see in
your eyes
shimmering the words *"i found magic"*
moments like those may last a lifetime
but many are not so lucky
it's like a quick high that no one can ever take
you to again
so weightless and free
you're happily lost
internal completion found internally in another
we can search for it in others
but it never compares
you'll always have that one moment
that rare appearance

in times like these, i can't help but think of you
when the light starts to flicker
and there's no one in the room
they say i've lost my mind
if you were here
you would say *"that's not like you"*
i can't help but think
was that you?


*forgive me, father*

i'll let this wind be a kiss from you
imagining that your wings created these waves
before you flew

to love one more than yourself is not a chore
it is a choice
your heart craving for someone to hear its roar
aching for someone to care for
waiting for the one who understands
that's the great war

*loving another*

remember to always trust that gut feeling
it will never do you wrong
let it be the judge in your ruling
let it guide your choosing
not all are worthy of pursuing

i know the feeling that you're having
the one that your being has been missing
the feeling of all the beating wings of the
butterflies in your stomach causing your lifting
i know, it's addicting
just make sure you don't dismiss the sound of a
snake hissing

i've become a ship at sea searching for a
lighthouse
a captain with no guide feeling every bit of
doubt
another bit of land to sail to i've crossed out
sailing all alone
so much to think about

after all the tears have dried
your chest will harbor a storm
whiskey, your preferable tide
followed by a horrid cold war
embrace the change inside
leading you to your new form

every new you will always be beautiful

waterline war paint

the new you

saying *"i miss you"* would be irrelevant
you never left
you became someone so much stronger
someone so much wiser than before
someone who finally figured out how much you
had to offer
i can't miss you when i am you


*the new you*

take it as a compliment when someone says that
you've changed
it only means you've grown

i've watered so many flower pots
wishing to see them grow
all while forgetting to water my own


*never again*

there's a part of me that i've shipped away
placed on a ship within a cargo box prepared for
high winds to set sail
i hear the desperate cries begging to be free
nails clawing at the walls
darling, that's your new home
i'll release you when there's someone worthy of
you to roam


*it's for your own good*

flora, the goddess of flowers
she brings along such precious favors
a stem filled with such great power
a gift one can savor
fields of mountains
filled with love in every color
born to feed a world full of hate
reminding us all hope exists
giving us all just a bit of flutter

yes, you cut me open and i began to spill
but i discovered so much more of me
the empty me began to fill

i cannot continue to give myself away
if i lose any more of who i am
eventually, i'll have nothing left and no will to
mend a soul that's only goal was to feel whole


*darling, you were never missing a piece*

the world will only see what you show them
until you accept yourself for who you are
you will never live the life you want
stop hiding in the shadows
the world deserves to see your beauty
fuck what it may think of you
who declared there's only one right way to live?
is there only one right way to die?

they'll be the one to remind you to say *"no tomatoes"* when you're ordering because they know you're just going to eat around them

*the one*

some say you lose a part of yourself to someone
every time you fall in love
i wonder what others have lost to me since they
all claimed to have loved me

never beg for someone to stay in your life
you'd only be helping them hold your heart
hostage with you providing the knife

something so beautiful, yet so fragile
its beauty breathless
the essence in the air once you pluck it
so intoxicating
leaves a shiver down your spine

there are those special ones
the ones you give by the dozen
for each flower gives a kiss
not too many, and not too much
the perfect amount
a customized bunch
you need no reason to hand one them
and nothing else to go along


*flowers speak the words we cannot find to say*

they didn't understand you couldn't be contained
one day your flame will ignite one's world
only then will you understand why all the others
burned


*darling, a spark like yours is called a flame*

the ones watching you pass through their skies
know of your beauty
they'll speak of you to others
    *"you were the best view"*

they're reminded of your shine during each
glimpse of grey you once tore through
you'll forever be a shooting star

sitting in this café, drinking my tea
the yellow on the walls bring such calmness
teaspoon clinking the walls of my cup
light sipping, avoiding the leafs that broke free
black, yet so sweet
who is this girl sitting alone in such relief?

yes, i am new
yet the old me can still be found beneath each
scar that i have accepted
on rare nights, i trace each one with my finger
to remind myself
a love like mine must be protected

to indulge in my ivory comes with a price
your fingers must play a breathless melody
empty notes will no longer suffice
i will no longer release my love so recklessly


*no longer my own enemy*

understand that you are not required to reply
they didn't feel the need to comfort you even
though they were the cause of your cries
   *"i miss you, stop being an ass"*


how rude of you to defy their goodbye

i write not only to heal
but to wear my words as a caution sign
that way they can never say they didn't know
what they were getting themselves into
i wrote it all out for you

this is me
this is who i am

i once was naïve and thought the world of
everyone brought to me
the reality that nobody is in control of my own
happiness was a struggle to achieve
the old me would be in disbelief

*i'm complete and it's just me*

waterline war paint

darling, never turn grey
i promise you that you'll be okay

just look at me today

waterline war paint

CPSIA information can be obtained
at www.ICGtesting.com
Printed in the USA
BVHW031946261018
531358BV00002B/79/P